BIPOLAR DISORDER
Living With Bipolar Disorder Patient & Managing Bipolar Disorder

Theresa Abraham

Table of contents

Chapter 1

ABOUT BIPOLAR DISORDER

A person with bipolar illness may experience fluctuations in mood, energy, and activity levels that can make day-to-day life challenging.

The bipolar disease may cause serious disruption to a person's life, although the effect differs across people. With adequate treatment and support, many persons with this illness live a full and active life.

According to the National Alliance on Mental Illness (NAMI), bipolar illness affects about 10 million individuals in the United States, or roughly 2.8% of the population.

On average, a person will acquire a diagnosis around the age of 25 years, however, symptoms might occur during the adolescent years or later in life. It affects men and females equally.

What Is Bipolar Disorder?

A person with bipolar illness may experience "highs" and "lows" in fast succession.
The National Institute of Mental Health identifies the basic symptoms of bipolar disorder as alternating spells of high and low mood. Changes in energy levels, sleep habits, capacity to concentrate, and other traits may

profoundly affect a person's behavior, job, relationships, and other parts of life.

Most individuals experience mood fluctuations at some point, but those connected to bipolar illness are more extreme than typical mood swings, and additional symptoms might develop. Some individuals suffer from psychosis, which may involve delusions, hallucinations, and paranoia.

Between episodes, the person's mood may remain stable for months or years, particularly if they are following treatment plans.

Treatment helps many individuals with bipolar illness to work, study, and enjoy a full and productive life. However, when therapy makes a person feel better, they may discontinue taking their medicine. Then, the symptoms might recur.

Some parts of bipolar illness may make a person feel fantastic. During an enhanced mood, individuals may discover they are more friendly, conversational, and creative.

However, a heightened mood is unlikely to endure. Even if it does, it may be challenging to maintain attention or follow through with goals. This might make it tough to follow a project through to the finish.

Symptoms

According to the International Bipolar Association, symptoms differ across people. For some individuals, an episode might linger for many months or years. Others may experience "highs" and "lows" at the same time or in fast succession.

In "rapid cycling" bipolar disorder, the individual will have four or more episodes within a year.

Mania or hypomania
Hypomania and mania are high emotions. Mania is more intense than hypomania.

Symptoms might include:
impaired judgment
feeling weird
sleeping little but not feeling tired
a sensation of distraction or boredom
missing work or school
underperforming at work or school
feeling able to do anything
being sociable and forthcoming, sometimes aggressively
engaging in risky behavior
increased libido
feeling exhilarated or euphoric
having high levels of self-confidence, self-esteem, and self-importance
talking a lot and rapidly
jumping from one topic to another in conversation
having "racing" thoughts that come and go quickly, and bizarre ideas that the person may act upon

denying or not realizing that anything is wrong
Some persons with bipolar illness may spend a lot of
money, take recreational drugs, drink alcohol, and
indulge in unsafe and inappropriate activities.

Depressive symptoms
During an episode of bipolar depression, a person may
experience:
a sense of gloom, sorrow, and hopelessness
severe sadness
insomnia and sleeping troubles
anxiousness over little matters
suffering or bodily issues that may not respond to
treatment
a feeling of shame, which may be misguided
eating more or eating less
weight loss or weight gain
severe weariness, lethargy, and listlessness
an incapacity to appreciate activities or hobbies that
ordinarily generate pleasure
difficulties concentrating and remembering
irritability
sensitivity to sounds, scents, and other things that
others may not notice\san inability to face going to work
or school, perhaps leading to underperformance
In extreme circumstances, the person may think about
terminating their life, and they may act on such ideas.

Psychosis

If a "high" or "low" episode is exceedingly severe, the individual may develop psychosis. They may have problems discriminating between dreams and reality.
According to the International Bipolar Foundation, psychosis symptoms during a high include hallucinations, which entail hearing or seeing things that are not there, and delusions, which are erroneous but deeply felt beliefs. A person who has delusions may feel they are famous, have high-ranking social connections, or have extraordinary abilities.

During a depressed or "low" phase, people may imagine they have committed a crime or are ruined and impoverished.

It is feasible to control all these symptoms with suitable therapy.

Bipolar disorder may also damage memory. Learn more here.

Types of bipolar disorder
A person may obtain a diagnosis of one of three basic categories of bipolar illness. According to NAMI, symptoms occur on a continuum, and the difference between the categories is not always clear-cut.

Bipolar I condition
For a diagnosis of bipolar I disorder:
The subject must have undergone at least one manic episode.

The individual may have experienced a past serious depressive episode.
The doctor must rule out other diseases, such as schizophrenia and delusional disorder.

Bipolar II disorder
Bipolar II illness features moments of hypomania, although depression is generally the dominating condition.

For a diagnosis of bipolar II disorder, a person must have had:
done or more bouts of depression
at least one hypomanic episode
no other diagnosis to explain the mood swings
A person with hypomania may feel well and perform well, but their mood may not be stable, and there is a danger that depression will follow.

People sometimes conceive of bipolar II disorder as a milder variant. For many, though, it is just different. As NAMI shows, persons with bipolar II condition may have more frequent periods of depression than those with bipolar I disease.

Cyclothymia
The National Health Service (NHS) in the United Kingdom states that cyclothymia shares comparable traits to bipolar illness, but the Diagnostic and Statistical Manual of Mental Disorders, 5th Edition (DSM-5)

defines it independently. It includes hypomania and despair, although the alterations are less dramatic.

Nevertheless, cyclothymia may impair a person's everyday life, and a doctor can give therapy.

The National Institute of Mental Health (NIMH) notes that to get a diagnosis of bipolar I disorder, a person must have experienced symptoms for at least 7 days, or fewer if symptoms were severe enough to necessitate hospitalization. They may have experienced a depressive episode lasting at least 2 weeks.

To acquire a diagnosis of bipolar II, a person will have undergone at least one cycle of hypomania and depression.

A doctor may carry out a physical examination and certain diagnostic procedures, including blood and urine tests, to help rule out other reasons.

It might be tough for a doctor to identify bipolar illness since patients are more likely to seek care in a low mood than in a good mood. As a consequence, it might be hard for them to differentiate it from depression.

If the individual has psychosis, a clinician may misdiagnose their condition as schizophrenia.

Other issues that may develop with bipolar illness are:
use of drugs or alcohol to deal with symptoms

post-traumatic stress disorder (PTSD)
anxiety disorder
attention-deficit hyperactivity disorder (ADHD)
NIMH recommends healthcare practitioners check for indicators of mania in the person's past, to avoid misdiagnosis. Some medications may provoke mania in vulnerable persons.

An individual who obtains a diagnosis of bipolar illness has a lifetime diagnosis. They may experience extended periods of stability, but they will always live with the disease.

Treatment
Treatment seeks to stabilize the person's mood and lessen the intensity of symptoms. The purpose is to assist the individual to operate properly in everyday life.

Treatment comprises a variety of treatments, including:
medication
counseling
physical intervention
lifestyle cures
It might take time to establish a precise diagnosis and find a good therapy since people respond differently, and symptoms vary greatly.

Drug treatment
Drug therapies may help stabilize mood and control symptoms. A doctor may typically prescribe a mix of:
mood stabilizers, such as lithium

antidepressants
second-generation antipsychotics (SGAs)
anticonvulsants, to reduce mania medication to aid with sleep or anxiety
The doctor may need to alter the dosage over time. Some medications have side effects, and they might affect people differently. If a person has concerns about their drug therapy, they should speak to their doctor.

A person must:
tell the doctor about any other drugs they are receiving, to limit the chance of interactions and unwanted effects
follow the doctor's directions about medication and therapy
express any concerns about ill effects, and whether they believe the therapy is working
continue taking medicine until the doctor advises it is safe to stop
bear in mind that the treatments may take time to act
If the individual discontinues therapy, symptoms may worsen.

Psychotherapy and counseling
Psychotherapy may help reduce symptoms and educate a person to manage bipolar illness.

Through cognitive-behavior therapy (CBT) and other treatments, the person may learn to:
recognize and take actions to control significant triggers, such as stress

notice early indicators of an episode and take actions to manage it

focus on variables that assist maintain a stable mood for as long as possible

engage the aid of family members, instructors, and coworkers

These actions may help a person maintain great connections at home and work. For children and teenagers with bipolar illness, a doctor may prescribe family therapy.

Hospital therapy
Some individuals may need to spend time in the hospital if there is a danger of them injuring themselves or others.

If previous treatments have not worked, a doctor may give electroconvulsive therapy (ECT).

Lifestyle remedies
Some lifestyle changes might help maintain a steady mood and control symptoms. They include:

maintaining a routine

following a balanced and diverse diet

establishing a regular sleep pattern and taking actions to minimize sleep interruption

obtaining regular exercise

Some individuals utilize supplements, however, it is vital to discuss this with a doctor beforehand. Some natural therapies may interact with the medicines used for bipolar illness. They may make symptoms worse.

Causes
Bipolar disorder seems to come from a variety of circumstances.

Genetic factors: Bipolar disorder is more likely in people who have a family member with the disease. A lot of genetic traits may be implicated.

Biological traits: Research shows that abnormalities in neurotransmitters or hormones that impact the brain may have a role.

Environmental factors: Life experiences, such as abuse, mental stress, a "significant loss," or another traumatic incident, may cause the first episode in a vulnerable individual.

Outlook
Bipolar illness is a reasonably common but dangerous mental health disease that includes swings in mood, energy levels, and attention, plus other symptoms.

It may significantly impair a person's life, but therapy can substantially improve the outlook.

Treatment may not remove mood fluctuations altogether, but working closely with a doctor may make symptoms more bearable and increase the quality of life.

What are some drugs for bipolar depression?

Standard therapy
Mood stabilizers
Antipsychotics
Antidepressants
Benzodiazepines

Summary

Bipolar disorder is a mental health illness that causes fluctuations in a person's mood, energy levels, focus, and ability to carry out everyday tasks. Bipolar depression is the depressed mood characteristic in persons with bipolar disorder. Medications may help control symptoms, regulate mood, and enhance overall well-being.

Bipolar disorder is a lifelong mental health problem. Many persons with the illness will need continual long-term therapy to control symptoms. Symptoms include high and low emotions, which are known as mania and depression.

A psychiatrist will offer drugs with other interventional therapy to treat bipolar depression.

What is the conventional therapy for bipolar depression? Medications are often the first-line therapy for bipolar depression. However, most treatment approaches incorporate a mix of medication, psychotherapy, and lifestyle adjustments.

A person's symptoms and kind of bipolar illness will dictate their therapy.

A person will likely get therapy for bipolar depression in an outpatient clinic setting. However, a person may be admitted to the hospital if their symptoms are severe and their risk of danger or self-harm is significant.

Medical and mental health specialists may prescribe drugs such as mood stabilizers, antipsychotics, and antidepressants.

Once a person's mood stabilizes as a consequence of their meds, they might pursue psychotherapy to learn how to manage their illness. This occurs throughout the maintenance phase of therapy. Also at this period, physicians provide drugs to avoid a recurrence.

People with bipolar depression may require more than one medicine to treat their symptoms. For instance, they may take a mood-stabilizing medicine coupled with an antipsychotic or antidepressant.

Because individuals react to drugs differently, it might take a long time for physicians to determine the appropriate prescription or combination to address each person's symptoms. To establish the optimal treatment approach, clinicians evaluate the following factors:
the intensity of a person's symptoms
any underlying health conditions
previous or present drugs

the safety and tolerability of the medicine and alternative therapeutic options
a person's treatment choice

Other therapies

Bipolar drugs may be most successful when patients take them with other therapies, such as the following:
Psychotherapy
According to a 2017 set of professional practice recommendations published in the Indian Journal of Psychiatry, psychotherapy may minimize the risk of relapse and enhance health outcomes throughout the acute and maintenance treatment periods of bipolar depression.

Psychotherapy includes one-on-one engagement with a therapist. Some examples of methods of psychotherapy are:
cognitive behavioral therapy
interpersonal and social rhythm treatment
family-focused treatment
Electroconvulsive treatment (ECT)
A doctor may consider ECT if a person's bipolar depression is severe and does not respond to medication and psychotherapy.

In this surgery, physicians will give a person general anesthesia before stimulating the brain with an electrical current.

Researchers in 2017 research investigated the effect of ECT on 522 patients with bipolar illness. Two-thirds of the participants had favorable results. The researchers found that ECT is safe and effective for treating all stages of severe, drug-resistant bipolar illness.

Lifestyle adjustments
Making good lifestyle choices may help avoid a return of bipolar depression. People may attempt the following approaches:
eating a balanced diet
avoiding drugs and alcohol
exercising regularly
getting appropriate rest
taking drugs according to their prescription
attending medical and mental health visits
People should continue taking their prescriptions even after their symptoms improve.

When to consult a doctor
A person should consult a doctor if they are having increasing symptoms or adverse effects while taking medication for bipolar illness.

The doctor may make occasional modifications by changing a medicine or lowering the dosage to address severe side effects. They will also monitor how a person's symptoms improve with each modification.

If a person does not observe quick improvements after commencing therapy for bipolar illness, they do not need to worry. It may take a while for them to start noticing major changes.

Outlook

The National Institute of Mental Health says that 2.8% of individuals in the United States have a bipolar disorder diagnosis. This corresponds to 5 million individuals. And 82.9% of these persons have a severe disability.

According to the United Kingdom's National Health Service (NHS), without therapy, bipolar-related mania might persist for 3–6 months and depression episodes can last 6–12 months.

The NHS also claims that symptoms normally improve after 3 months of treatment, which includes medication, psychotherapy, and lifestyle modifications.

Summary
There is presently no treatment for bipolar depression. However, therapy may help a person manage the illness.

A person's doctor will recommend a combination of medications, psychosocial interventions, and lifestyle changes for maximum effect.

People with bipolar depression should work closely with a doctor and follow their prescribed treatment plan to have the best

Chapter 2

WHAT IS DEPRESSION?

Everyone may feel melancholy or stressed at times. But depression is a persistent sensation of emptiness, sorrow, or inability to enjoy a pleasure that may seem to come for no evident cause. It is separate from sadness and other feelings a person may experience after painful life situations.

Depression is the largest cause of disability globally, according to the World Health Organization (WHO).

It may weaken a person's relationships, making working and keeping good health extremely difficult, and in severe situations, may lead to suicide. Depression correlates to over 40,000 suicides in the United States each year.

It may impact adults, adolescents, and children. This page explores what depression is and what causes it, as well as forms of depression, treatment, and more.

What Is Depression?
Depression is a mood illness that produces persistent feelings of sorrow, emptiness, and lack of joy. It is distinct from the mood changes that individuals constantly encounter as a part of life.

Major life experiences, such as bereavement or the loss of a career, may precipitate depression. But depression is separate from the bad sensations a person may momentarily experience in reaction to a traumatic life event.

Depression typically endures despite a change of circumstances and creates sensations that are severe, persistent, and not proportionate to a person's circumstances.

It is a continuing issue, not a fleeting one. While there are numerous forms of depression, the most frequent one is a major depressive disorder. It comprises episodes during which the symptoms linger for at least two weeks.

Depression may linger for many weeks, months, or years. For many individuals, it is a chronic sickness that gets better and then relapses.

Is it curable?
While there is no cure for depression, there are effective therapies that aid in rehabilitation. The sooner that therapy begins, the more effective it may be. Some individuals may never experience depression again after a single bout of it. Others will continue to suffer relapses.

Many persons with depression recover following a treatment regimen. Even with excellent therapy, though, a recurrence may occur. About half of people do not immediately react to the therapy.

To avoid recurrence, persons who take medication for depression should continue with therapy — even when symptoms improve or go away — for as long as their doctor suggests.

Signs and Symptoms
Depression may induce several psychological and physical symptoms, including:
prolonged sad mood
loss of interest or pleasure in hobbies and activities
changes in eating and body weight
abnormally slow or frantic motions
low energy or weariness
difficulties sleeping or oversleeping
excessive emotions of shame or worthlessness
difficulty concentrating or making decisions
thoughts of death or suicide, or suicide attempts
If a person suffers five or more of these symptoms throughout the same 2-week period, a doctor may diagnose them with depression.

Depression may also produce other symptoms, including irritability, restlessness, chronic pain, headaches, and digestive difficulties.

Types of depression

There are numerous varieties of depression. Below are some of the most prevalent varieties.

Major depression
A person dealing with serious depression has a continual sense of melancholy. They may lose interest in activities they used to like.

Treatment generally includes medication and psychotherapy.

Persistent depressive disorder
Also known as dysthymia, persistent depressive illness produces symptoms that endure for at least 2 years.

A person living with this condition may experience bouts of severe depression as well as lesser symptoms that may not fulfill the criteria for major depressive disorder.

Postpartum depression
After giving delivery, some women experience a short time of melancholy or heightened emotions that some people term the "baby blues." This normally fades away in a few days to a few weeks.
Postpartum depression, or postnatal depression, is more severe.
There is no one reason for this sort of depression, and it may last for months or years. Anyone who develops prolonged depression after delivery should seek medical assistance.

Major depressive disorder with seasonal pattern
Previously known as seasonal affective disorder (SAD), this kind of depression usually occurs during the winter and autumn months, when there is less daylight. Less occasionally, it may follow other seasonal patterns.

It lifts over the remainder of the year and in response to light treatment.

This illness tends to mainly affect persons who reside in nations with long or harsh winters.

What causes depression?
The medical profession does not completely grasp the causes of depression. There are numerous probable reasons, and occasionally, many things combine to induce symptoms.

Factors that are likely to have a role include:
genetic traits
changes in the brain's neurotransmitter levels
environmental variables such as exposure to stress or lack of social support
psychological and social aspects
other conditions, such as bipolar disorder
Interactions between several variables might raise the likelihood of depression. For instance, a person with a family history or a genetic susceptibility to depression may have signs of depression after a distressing incident.

The symptoms of depression can include:

a depressed mood
reduced interest or pleasure in activities that a person
previously enjoyed loss of sexual desire
changes in appetite
unintentional weight loss or gain
sleeping too much or too little
agitation, restlessness, and pacing up and down
slowed movement and speech
fatigue or loss of energy
feelings of worthlessness or guilt
difficulty thinking, concentrating or making decisions
recurrent thoughts of death or suicide, or an attempt at
suicide

In females
Depression is approximately twice as frequent in girls as
in men, according to the Centers for Disease Control and
Prevention (CDC).
Researchers do not know why depression seems to be
more frequent among females. However, 2021 research
indicates that the gap may be due to differences in
reporting. Researchers showed that females were more
likely than males to report and seek treatment for
depressive symptoms.
Some study shows that exposure to gender
discrimination increases the risk of depression.
Also, certain kinds of depression are exclusive to
females, such as postpartum depression and
premenstrual dysphoric disorder.

In males

According to statistics from the National Health and Nutrition Survey, which focuses on self-reports of mental health symptoms, 5.5% of males experience depressive symptoms in a given 2-week period, compared with 10.4% of females.

Males with depression are more prone than females to consume alcohol in excess, express aggression, and participate in risk-taking as a consequence of the disease.

Other signs of depression in guys may include:

avoiding family and social situations

working without a break

having difficulties keeping up with work and family responsibilities

displaying harsh or dominating behavior in relationships

In college students

Time at college may be difficult, and a person may be coping with various lives, cultures, and experiences for the first time.

Some kids have difficulties dealing with these changes, and they may develop sadness, anxiety, or both as a consequence.

Symptoms of depression among college students may include:

difficulties focusing on schoolwork

insomnia

sleeping too much

a loss or increase in appetite

avoiding social settings and activities that they used to like

In teenagers

Physical changes, social pressure, and other factors might lead to depression in adolescence.

They may encounter some of the following symptoms:
feeling irritable
restlessness, such as an inability to sit still withdrawing from friends and family difficulty focusing on school work
feeling guilty, powerless, or worthless
In children
The CDC estimates that, in the U.S., 4.4% of children and teens aged 3–17 had a diagnosis of depression. This number has climbed in recent years.

Depression in youngsters may make schooling and social activities tough. They may suffer symptoms such as:
crying
low energy
clinginess
defiant conduct
vocal eruptions
Younger children may have difficulties expressing how they feel in language. This might make it tougher for them to convey their emotions of grief.

In historically disadvantaged groups
Research suggests that the frequency of serious depression among African Americans has been

approximately 10.4%, compared with 17.9% among persons who are white.

However, 56% of African Americans suffer depression more persistently, compared with 38.6% of those who are white. This means that whereas fewer African Americans may suffer depression, those who do may endure it for longer. In addition, less than half of these African Americans have sought treatment.

Other study shows that African Americans may suffer depression less commonly than non-Hispanic persons who are white, although this may be related to the fact that many African Americans often do not get a thorough diagnosis.

Triggers
Triggers are emotional, psychological, or physical events or conditions that might cause depression symptoms to arise or recur.
These are some of the most typical triggers:
significant life situations, such as death, family strife, and changes in relationships
incomplete recovery after having discontinued depression medication too soon
medical illnesses, particularly a medical crisis such as a new diagnosis or a chronic ailment such as heart disease or diabetes

Risk factors

Some people have a greater risk of depression than others.

Risk factors include:

experiencing particular life events, such as bereavement, employment challenges, changes in relationships, financial problems, and medical concerns

enduring intense stress

having a lack of effective coping techniques

having a close family with depression

using certain prescription medicines, such as corticosteroids, some beta-blockers, and interferon

using recreational substances, such as alcohol or amphetamines

having incurred a head injury

having a neurological condition such as Alzheimer's or Parkinson's\shaving experienced a prior bout of significant depression

having a chronic ailment, such as diabetes, chronic obstructive pulmonary disease (COPD), or cardiovascular disease

living with chronic pain

lacking social support

Depression as a symptom

Depression may also emerge as a symptom or comorbidity with another mental health issue. Examples include:

Psychotic depression

Psychosis may entail delusions, such as mistaken beliefs and a disconnection from reality. It may also entail hallucinations – perceiving things that do not exist.

Some individuals suffer from depression alongside psychosis. A person living with psychosis, which is a severe mental disorder, may develop depression as a consequence.

Alternatively, a person suffering from depression may have a severe form of the disorder that also involves psychotic symptoms.

Bipolar disorder
Depression is a typical symptom of bipolar illness. People with bipolar illness undergo episodes of depression that may last weeks. They also have bouts of mania, which is a heightened mood that may lead a person to feel highly euphoric, violent, or out of control.

Treatment
Depression is curable, albeit the therapy may vary on the precise form a person is living with.

However, roughly 30.9% of persons do not react to therapy or respond badly. About 4 in 10 patients obtain remission of their symptoms within 12 months, however, depression might come back.

Managing symptoms usually includes three components:
Support: This might vary from addressing practical solutions and probable reasons to educating family members.

Psychotherapy: Also known as talking therapy, some possibilities include one-to-one counseling and cognitive behavioral therapy(CBT).

Drug treatment: A doctor may prescribe antidepressants.

Medication

Antidepressants may help treat mild to severe depression. Several classes of antidepressants are available:

selective serotonin reuptake inhibitors (SSRIs)

selective serotonin and norepinephrine reuptake inhibitors(SNRIs)

typical antidepressants tricyclic antidepressants monoamine oxidase inhibitors(MAOIs)

Each class acts on a different neurotransmitter or combination of neurotransmitters.

A person should only take these medications as their doctor prescribes. Some drugs can take a while to have an impact. By stopping taking the drug, a person may not experience the benefits that it can offer.

Some people stop taking medication after symptoms improve, but this can lead to a relapse.

A person should raise any concerns about antidepressants with a doctor, including any intention to stop taking the medication.

Medication side effects

SSRIs and SNRIs can have side effects. A person may experience:

nausea

constipation

diarrhea

low blood sugar

weight loss or weight gain

a rash

sexual dysfunction

The Food and Drug Administration (FDA) requires manufacturers to put a "black box" warning on antidepressant bottles.

The warning emphasizes that, among other hazards, these drugs may increase suicidal thoughts or acts in certain adolescents, teens, and young adults during the first few months of therapy. While there is an increase in danger, the absolute risk remains minimal.

Natural Remedies

Some individuals utilize natural therapies, such as herbal medications, to treat mild to severe depression.

However, because the FDA does not oversee herbal cures, producers may not be genuine about the quality of these items. They may not be safe or effective.

In a 2018 systematic review of herbal medicines for depression, 45% of trials showed excellent outcomes from herbal treatments, including fewer adverse effects than mainstream antidepressants.

The following are some of the more prominent herbs and plants that people use to alleviate depression:
Ginseng: Practitioners of traditional treatment may utilize this to increase mental clarity and relieve stress. Find out more about ginseng here.
Chamomile: This includes flavonoids that may have an antidepressant impact. For additional information about chamomile, go here.
Lavender: This may help relieve anxiety and sleeplessness. Learn more about lavender here.
A person must consult with a doctor before utilizing any form of herbal cure or supplement to treat depression. Some herbs may interfere with the action of medications or otherwise make symptoms worse.

Supplements
A person may use the herbs above as supplements to alleviate symptoms of mild to moderate depression. Other sorts of vitamins may also help relieve similar symptoms.

It is vital to note that the FDA does not regulate supplements to guarantee that they are beneficial or safe.

Non Herbal supplements that may help alleviate depression include S-adenosylmethionine (SAMe) – a synthetic version of a natural molecule in the body. They also contain 5-hydroxytryptophan, which may aid to enhance serotonin, the neurotransmitter in the brain that impacts a person's mood.

Some study has shown that SAMe may be as useful as the prescription antidepressants imipramine and escitalopram, but additional examination is recommended.

Food and Diet
Some evidence shows that consuming a lot of sugary or processed meals might contribute to different physical health issues and poor mental health. Results of 2019 research revealed that a diet that comprises lots of these sorts of food may impair the mental health of young people.

The research also revealed that consuming more of the following items helps lower depressive symptoms:
fruit
vegetables
fish
olive oil

Psychotherapy
Psychotherapy, or talking treatments, for depression include CBT, interpersonal psychotherapy, and problem-solving treatment.

For certain kinds of depression, psychotherapy is frequently the first-line treatment, whereas other individuals react better to a combination of psychotherapy and medicines.

CBT and interpersonal psychotherapy are the two basic kinds of psychotherapy for depression. A person may receive CBT in individual sessions with a therapist, in groups, over the telephone, or online.

CBT focuses on helping a person discover the relationship between their ideas, actions, and emotions. They then strive methodically to modify damaging beliefs and habits.

Interpersonal therapy seeks to help patients identify:
emotional difficulties that impair relationships and communication
how these issues also affect their mood
ways to strengthen relationships and better control emotions
Exercise
Aerobic exercise improves endorphin levels and activates neurotransmitters, possibly relieving sadness and anxiety. A 2019 article says that exercise may be particularly effective for treatment-resistant depression.

Exercise delivers the greatest advantages when a person mixes it with traditional therapies, such as antidepressants and psychotherapy.

Brain stimulation therapy

Brain stimulation therapies are another therapy option. For example, repeated transcranial magnetic stimulation transmits magnetic pulses to the brain, and this may help cure serious depression.

If depression does not respond to pharmacological treatment, a person may benefit from electroconvulsive therapy(ECT). Doctors do not completely grasp how ECT works.

During the operation, a person is sleeping, and a doctor uses electricity to cause a seizure. This may help "reset" the brain, fixing abnormalities with neurotransmitters or other disorders that underlie sadness.

Diagnosis
If a person believes that they have signs of depression, they should get professional care from a doctor or mental health expert.

A qualified health professional can rule out various causes, ensure an accurate diagnosis, and provide safe and effective treatment.

They will ask questions about symptoms, such as how long they have been present. A doctor may also conduct an examination to check for physical causes and order a blood test to rule out other health conditions.

Tests

Mental health professionals often ask people to complete questionnaires to help assess the severity of their depression.

Is depression genetic?
A person with a parent or sibling who has depression is about three times more likely than other people to develop the condition.

However, many people with depression have no family history of it.

A recent study suggests that susceptibility to depression may not result from genetic variation. The researchers acknowledge that while people can inherit depression, many other issues also influence its development.

Is it a disability?
Depression is the leading cause of disability around the world, according to the WHO.

In the U.S., the Social Security Administration considers depressive, bipolar, and related disorders to be disabilities. If a person's depression prevents them from working, they may qualify for social security disability insurance benefits.

The person must have worked long enough and recently enough to qualify for disability benefits. For further information, check the administration's website.

Statistics

According to the CDC, around 11% of physician office visits reflect depression on the medical record. The figure is comparable for emergency department visits.

Also according to the CDC, 4.4% of children and adolescents between the ages of 3 and 17 years — nearly 2.7 million individuals in the U.S. — have a diagnosis of depression.

The CDC also says that 4.7% of American adults suffer frequent symptoms of depression.

What does depression do to the brain?
Depression may lead to changes in levels of neurotransmitters, which are chemicals that convey information between nerve cells. In the long term, it may also cause physical changes to the brain, including decreases in gray matter volume and increased inflammation.

Does melancholy affect your personality?
Research has thrown up varied conclusions concerning whether or not depression may genuinely modify a person's personality.

However, according to one evaluation of 10 research, depressive symptoms may be connected with changes in numerous particular components of personality — including extraversion, neuroticism, and agreeableness — which might be transitory or lasting.

Does depression impact your thinking?
Depression may affect focus and decision-making. It may also decrease focus and create difficulty with information processing and memory.

Summary

Depression is a serious, chronic medical condition that can affect every aspect of a person's life. When it causes suicidal thoughts, it can be fatal.

People cannot reason their way out of despair. Depression is neither a personal shortcoming nor a sign of weakness. It is curable, and obtaining therapy early may boost the odds of recovery.

Because depression may be tough to cure, it is necessary for a person to consult a doctor with knowledge of depression and to be prepared to try multiple different therapies. Often, a combination of treatment and medicine produces the greatest outcomes.

Chapter 3

HOW TO LIVE WITH BIPOLAR PATIENT

Assisting Someone With Bipolar Disorder
Adapting to a friend or family member's bipolar illness is difficult. This lead will assist you with arranging the trouble and help your companion or relative.
What might you do for somebody with bipolar disorder?
Adapting to the high points and low points of bipolar problems might be troublesome — and not only for the person with the sickness. The feelings and activities of an individual with bipolar infections influence everybody around — particularly relatives and dear companions. It might put a heap on your relationship and upset many pieces of day-to-day life.

During a hyper episode, you might need to make unsafe moves, excessive requests, hazardous agents, and hasty decisions. Furthermore, after the tempest of frenzy has subsided, it regularly falls on you to adapt to the results. During seasons of melancholy, you might need to blame a friend or family member who doesn't have the energy to satisfy commitments at home or work.

Fortunately, most people with the bipolar ailment can settle their states of mind with proper treatment, prescription, and backing. Your understanding, empathy, and understanding might play a crucial job in your cherished one's treatment and recuperation. Frequently, having somebody to talk to may have a significant effect on their mentality and drive.

Yet, focusing on an individual with bipolar sickness may likewise incur significant damage on the off chance that you overlook your necessities, so finding some kind of harmony between aiding your cherished one and dealing with yourself is critical.

Different techniques to assist somebody with bipolar ailment
You may likewise support your cherished one by:

Finding out about bipolar sickness. Realize all you can about the side effects and treatment choices. The more you are familiar with bipolar sickness, the more ready you'll be to help your loved one and keep things in context.

Encouraging the person to get help. The sooner bipolar disease is dealt with, the better the chance, so urge your loved one to move into master care quickly. Try not to hold on to see whether they will get better without treatment.

Be understanding. Tell your companion or relative that you're free on the off chance that they need a reassuring ear, back, or help with treatment. Individuals with bipolar sickness often postpone getting help since they would rather not appear to be a burden to other people, so guarantee the individual that you give it a second thought and that you'll do anything you can to help.

Showing persistence. Getting solid takes time, in any event when an individual is dedicated to treatment. Try not to expect a speedy recovery or an extremely durable fix. Show restraint toward the pace of recuperating and prepare for difficulties and obstructions. Overseeing bipolar sickness is a lifetime venture.

The significance of help in bipolar confusion recuperation
Individuals with bipolar disorder improve when they have support from relatives and companions. They will quite often recuperate all the more rapidly, experience fewer hyper and burdensome episodes, and have milder side effects.

Bipolar disorder and the family
Residing with a bipolar individual can cause pressure and strain in the home. On top of the test of managing your loved one's side effects and their results, relatives frequently battle with sensations of culpability, dread, outrage, and vulnerability. Finally, the pressure can cause serious relationship issues. In any case, there are better ways of adapting.

The initial step to effectively managing bipolar disorder is for families to figure out how to acknowledge the ailment and its difficulties. While you're feeling crushed or regretful, recall that bipolar disorder isn't anybody's shortcoming. Tolerating bipolar disorder includes recognizing that things might, in all likelihood, at absolutely no point in the future be "ordinary."

Treatment can significantly impact your loved one, but it may not deal with all side effects or inabilities. To stay away from frustration and disdain, having practical suppositions is significant. Expecting a lot from your relatives can be a recipe for disappointment. Then again, expecting too little can likewise hinder their recuperation, so attempt to track down a harmony between encouraging freedom and offering help.

Ways to adapt to bipolar turmoil in the family
Acknowledge your loved one's cutoff points. Your loved one with bipolar disorder has zero control over their mindset. They can't simply wake up from melancholy or get a grip during a manic episode. Neither discouragement nor madness can be toppled through poise, self-discipline, or thinking. So telling your adored one to "Quit acting insane" or to "Look on the bright side" won't help.

Acknowledge your cutoff points. You can't save your adored one with bipolar turmoil, nor could you at any point prompt them to assume a sense of ownership with improvement. You can offer help, but in the long run, recuperation is in the possession of the individual with the disease.

Lower pressure. Stress exacerbates bipolar turmoil, so attempt to track down ways of diminishing pressure in your loved one's life. Ask how you can help and elect to assume control over a portion of the individual's liabilities if necessary. Laying out and implementing an everyday schedule — with ordinary times for getting up, having feasts, and heading to sleep — can likewise diminish family stress.

Impart straightforwardly. Transparent correspondence is vital for adapting to bipolar turmoil in the family. Share your interests in a caring manner, ask your cherished one how they're feeling, and try to genuinely tune in—regardless of whether you can't help contradicting your adored one or don't connect with what's being said.

Supporting an individual with bipolar confusion
What you can say that makes a difference:

"You're in good company in this. I'm hanging around for you. "
"I figure out that your ailment causes these considerations and sentiments."
"You may not trust it now, but how you're feeling can and will change."
"I will most likely be unable to see precisely the way that you feel, yet I care about you and need to help and support you."
"You mean quite a bit to me. "Your life means quite a bit to me."

Persuading an individual with bipolar turmoil to see a specialist

Besides offering daily encouragement, the most effective way to assist your loved one with bipolar disorder is by empowering and supporting treatment. Frequently, that can be, to a greater extent, a test than it sounds. Since individuals with bipolar confusion will quite often need an understanding of their condition, getting them to a doctor is difficult 100% of the time. When your cherished one is hyper, they feel perfect and don't understand there's an issue. At the point when your cherished one is discouraged, they might perceive something's off-base, yet frequently come up short on energy to look for help.

On the off chance that your adored one will not recognize the chance of bipolar disorder, don't quarrel over it. The thought might be alarming to them, so be delicate. All things being equal, or a specialist's visit for a particular side effect, like sleep deprivation, crabbiness, or weakness — then secretly call ahead to educate the specialist of your interests regarding bipolar disorder.

Things you can say that could be useful:

"Bipolar disorder" is a genuine disease, similar to diabetes. It requires clinical treatment. "
"You're not at fault for bipolar confusion. You didn't cause it. It's not your issue. "
"You can feel it improving. Numerous medicines can help."

"At the point when a bipolar issue isn't dealt with, it, as a rule, deteriorates."

Supporting a friend or family member during bipolar confusion treatment

When your companion or relative consents to seeing a specialist, you can help by being an accomplice in treatment. Your help can have a major effect on their treatment achievement, so propose to be engaged in a way your cherished one needs or needs.

Things you can do to help a friend or family member's bipolar disorder treatment:

Track down qualified specialists and advisors.
Set up arrangements and come.
Offer your experience to the specialist.
Screen your adored one's temperament.
Find out about their meds.
Track their treatment progress.
Watch for indications of a backslide.
Alert the specialist to issues.
Urge your beloved one to take bipolar disorder medicine.

Prescription is the foundation of treatment for bipolar confusion, and the vast majority need it to control their temperaments and stay away from backslides. Regardless of the requirement for medicine, many individuals with bipolar disorder quit taking it. Some quit because they're feeling improved, others on account of incidental effects, and still others since they partake in the side effects of madness. Individuals who don't think they have an issue are especially liable to quit taking drugs.

You can assist your beloved one remain focused by underlining the significance of drugs and ensuring they accept all remedies as coordinated. Additionally, urge your loved one to address their primary care physician about any troublesome incidental effects.

Optional impacts can be very unwanted if the piece of the medication is too low or too high, yet a change in the solution or estimations could handle the issue. Remind your loved one that abruptly stopping medication is dangerous.

Watch for cautioning indications of bipolar disorder relapse.
Regardless of whether your loved one with bipolar disorder is focused on treatment, there might be times when their side effects deteriorate. Make a move immediately if you notice any upsetting side effects or state of mind changes. Direct out the arising bipolar side effects toward your loved one and caution the specialist. With quick intercession, you might have the option of completely forestalling an episode of lunacy or misery from developing.

Try not to think about bipolar side effects literally. At that point, amidst a bipolar episode, individuals frequently say or do things that are pernicious or humiliating. When manic, your adored one might be wild, awful, basic, and forceful. When discouraged, they might be peevish, antagonistic, and touchy. It's hard not to think about such ways of behaving literally, but rather attempt to recall that they're side effects of your cherished one's dysfunctional behavior, not the aftereffect of narrow-mindedness or youthfulness.

Be ready for a disastrous way of behaving. When hyper or discouraged, individuals with bipolar disorder might act in damaging or flippant ways. Preparing for how to deal with such a way of behaving can help. When your cherished one is well, arrange a treatment plan that gives you advance endorsement to safeguard them when side effects show up. Settle on unambiguous advances you'll take, for example, eliminating Visas or vehicle keys, going together to the specialist, or assuming responsibility for family funds.

You are supporting somebody who is manic.

Invest energy with your adored one. Hyper individuals frequently feel disconnected from others. Investing even brief times of energy with them makes a difference. If your beloved one has a ton of energy, walk together. This allows your beloved one to keep progressing yet share your organization.

Answer questions sincerely. Be that as it may, don't contend or banter with somebody during a manic episode. Attempt to keep away from the extreme discussion.

Think about no remarks literally. During manic episodes, your loved one might say or do unusual things, remembering that they are centering on the negative parts of others. Attempt to stay away from contention.

Plan simple-to-eat feasts and beverages. It's frequently challenging for somebody who is hyper to plunk down to a feast, so have a go at offering them sandwiches, apples, cheddar saltines, and juices, for instance.

Try not to expose your precious one to a great deal of action and excitement. Keeping the environmental elements as calm as possible may be better.
Permit your cherished one to rest whenever the situation allows. During times of high energy, resting is troublesome. However, short rests required over the day can help. A hyper here and a hyper there, an individual might feel rested after a couple of long stretches of rest.

Dealing with yourself when a friend or family member has bipolar disorder
It's not difficult to disregard your own needs while you're supporting somebody with dysfunctional behavior. In any case, if you don't deal with yourself, you risk burnout — and that won't help you or your cherished one. When you deal with yourself both genuinely and actually, you'll have the option to all the more likely adapt to the pressure of really focusing on somebody with bipolar disorder and have the energy you want to help your loved one's recuperation.

Center around your own life. Supporting your cherished one might include some life changes, but ensure you don't neglect to focus on your objectives and needs. Try not to surrender kinship, plans, or exercises that give you pleasure.

Look for help. Managing a friend or family member's psychological instability can be difficult and stressful. Ensure you're getting the basic reassurance you want to adapt to. Converse with somebody you trust about the thing you're going through. It can, likewise, assist with seeking your treatment or joining a care group.

Put down stopping points. Be reasonable about how much consideration you're ready to give without feeling overpowered and angry. Put down certain boundaries on the thing you're willing and ready to do, and stick to them. Allowing bipolar turmoil to assume control over your life isn't good for you or your loved one.

Oversee pressure. Stress negatively affects the body and brain, so track down ways of holding it under control. Ensure you're eating right and getting sufficient rest and exercise. You can likewise monitor stress by rehearsing strategies like reflection.

Chapter 4

HEALTHY LIFESTYLE TIPS FOR MANAGING BIPOLAR DISORDER

There's a great deal you can do to assist with dealing with your bipolar problem. Alongside seeing your PCP and specialist and taking your medications, straightforward day-to-day propensities can have an effect.

Begin with these techniques.

Set a timetable. Many individuals with bipolar confusion find on the off chance that they adhere to a day-to-day plan, it assists them with controlling their state of mind.

Focus on your rest. This is particularly significant for individuals with bipolar disorder. Being sleepless can, in some cases, trigger craziness in those with the condition. It can likewise be an indication of an eruption of your side effects. For example, only a couple of evenings of less rest might imply that a hyper episode could come on. Or, on the other hand, if you begin to rest much more than usual, it could mean you're discouraged.

Utilize these tips:
Nod off and get up at similar times consistently.

Unwind before bed by paying attention to relieving music, perusing, or washing up.
Try not to sit up in bed staring at the TV or looking at your telephone.
Make your room a quiet space.
Assuming your rest patterns begin to change, tell your PCP or specialist.

Work out. It might further develop your state of mind whether you have bipolar confusion. You'll most likely sleep better, as well.

If you're not dynamic presently, check with your PCP that you're sufficiently sound to begin. Keep it basic from the start, like strolling with a companion. Bit by bit, work up to turning out for something like 30 minutes daily on most days of the week.

Eat well. There's no particular eating routine for individuals with bipolar confusion. However, very much like any other individual, picking the right sorts of food varieties can help you feel improved and give you the supplements you want. Center around the essentials: Favor natural products, vegetables, lean protein, and whole grains. Also, cut down on fat, salt, and sugar.

Tame pressure. Uneasiness can have deteriorating temperamental side effects in many individuals with bipolar disorder. To find an opportunity to unwind.

Lying on the loveseat staring at the TV or checking your web-based entertainment accounts isn't the most effective way to go. All things considered, take a stab at something more engaging, similar to yoga or different sorts of activity. Contemplation is another great decision. A simple method for doing that is to just zero in on your relaxation for a couple of moments, allowing different considerations to travel every which way without giving them a ton of consideration.

You can likewise pay attention to music or invest energy with positive individuals who are great organizations.

Make changes at home and work. Are there distressing things in your day-to-day existence that you could change? Whether it's in your family or at work, search for arrangements.

For example, might your accomplice at some point deal with a greater number of errands at home? Might your supervisor have the option to eliminate a portion of your obligations on the off chance that you're overburdened? Give your very best to improve your life and make it more straightforward.

Limit caffeine. It can keep you up around suppertime and potentially influence your mindset. So don't drink a ton of pop, espresso, or tea. Also, resist the urge to stress about chocolate, since it has caffeine. You could get rid of these things. It's not unexpected to do that bit by bit so you don't get cerebral pains and different indications of caffeine withdrawal.

Stay away from liquor and drugs. They can influence how your prescriptions work. They can likewise demolish bipolar confusion and trigger a mindset episode. Furthermore, they can make the condition harder to treat. So don't utilize them by any means.

Bipolar disorder can be a ton to manage. Many individuals go to liquor or medications and have a substance misuse issue.

On the off chance that you imagine that you generally disapprove of liquor or different medications, get help now. Bipolar treatment may not be sufficient. Substance misuse frequently needs a different treatment. You might have to handle the two circumstances simultaneously.

Exercise And Bipolar Disorder
Bipolar confusion is an emotional wellness condition that can cause low, burdensome moods and high, hyperactive temperaments. While the vast majority have gentle changes in the state of mind now and again, for individuals with bipolar disorder, these changes in temperament can be outrageous and flighty.

Bipolar confusion is regularly dealt with by prescription and treatment. Nonetheless, studies have shown that for certain individuals, adding activity to their treatment plan can provide added benefits. Peruse on to more deeply study the impact that exercise can have on bipolar confusion.

Exercise And Mood Challenges Of Bipolar Disorder

For the vast majority, exercise can emphatically affect their state of mind. When you work out, your body discharges endorphins, which are known as the mind's "vibe great" synthetics. After some time, more significant levels of endorphins can cheer you up. For this reason, practice is frequently suggested for individuals with gloom. Exercise can likewise assist you with combatting pressure.

Due to these advantages, it's not difficult to expect that working out could assist individuals with bipolar disorder. A survey of concentrates in 2015 found that they can be valid — yet not dependably so.

For example, one concentration in the survey found that for certain individuals with bipolar confusion, the practice helped ease hypomanic side effects, which are less serious than hypomanic side effects. It additionally assisted individuals with resting better. Furthermore, the review demonstrated the way that specific activities could have a calming impact on certain individuals. These activities incorporate strolling, running, and swimming.

Nonetheless, that equivalent review noticed that for others with bipolar turmoil, exercise could worsen manic side effects. It could cause a declining "spiraling" impact for both manic and hypomanic episodes.

Different examinations have tracked down comparative outcomes. In one review from 2013, scientists developed a program that consolidated activity, nourishment, and well-being preparation for overweight individuals with bipolar disorder. They noticed that the program brought about upgrades in well-being and weight. It additionally decreased the side effects of despondency in members and worked on their general work. In any case, they noticed that their outcomes likewise showed that exercise could reduce hypertension side effects.

Exercise And The Health Risk Of Bipolar Disorder
Bipolar confusion can influence something beyond your mindset. On the off chance that you have this condition, you're at a higher risk for other well-being concerns.

Research in 2015 showed that assuming you have bipolar turmoil, you might have a higher chance of medical issues. For example,

Heaviness

stroke

Coronary illness

Type 2 diabetes

The examination likewise showed that, besides the fact that these medical issues are a worry for your general well-being, they may likewise increase your side effects of bipolar problems.

A potential justification for these expanded well-being gambles is the expanded inactive way of behaving (non-active work) related to the condition. A 2017 investigation of individuals living with psychological sickness observed that they were more stationary than individuals without dysfunctional behavior. What's more, of those with psychological maladjustment, individuals with bipolar turmoil were the most sedentary.

Sedentary behavior can lessen your chance of getting or demolishing these other medical conditions related to bipolar confusion. It can assist you with dealing with your weight and diminish your chances of stroke, coronary illness, and type 2 diabetes.

Exercise and weight gain from prescriptions for bipolar confusion
As indicated above, corpulence can be an issue for individuals with bipolar confusion. In a portion of these cases, the weight gain could be brought about by the utilization of specific prescriptions for bipolar confusion. The prescriptions might cause metabolic changes that keep your body from consuming calories as efficiently as it did previously. Or, on the other hand, the medications could essentially increase your craving.

The following sorts of prescriptions might cause weight gain:
Antidepressants
antipsychotics
Energizer antipsychotic blends
state of mind stabilizers

Assuming you observe that you're out of nowhere putting on weight in the wake of beginning any of these prescriptions, converse with your primary care physician. On the off chance that you have uncontrolled weight gain, you might have to attempt an alternate prescription. Be that as it may, don't take constantly changing prescriptions or change your measurements without first talking with your primary care physician.

In different cases, increasing how much activity you do, in all actuality, could assist you with getting more fit. Practice consumes calories and can build muscle, both of which can assist you with shedding pounds.

Standpoint
Bipolar confusion is a long-lasting condition, but it very well may be made do with legitimate treatment. While a prescription is ordinarily the essential treatment choice for bipolar confusion, exercise can help as well. Generally speaking, it can assist with diminishing the side effects of bipolar problems as well as decrease the expanded risk of specific medical issues related to bipolar confusion.

For individuals with bipolar confusion, the Anxiety and Depression Association of America suggests working out for 30 minutes, 3 to 5 days out of every week. So, converse with your primary care physician about including exercise in your treatment plan. What's more, make certain to do the following:

Check with your primary care physician before beginning another activity routine, particularly if you're new to working out.

Stop any movement that causes torment or any deterioration in side effects and contact your primary care physician.

Make certain to converse with your primary care physician on the off chance that you notice that your hyper side effects increment in the wake of beginning another workout practice.

Work with your primary care physician to find the right activity plan for you, remembering that various sorts of activities work for various individuals. Attempt various choices until you find the arrangement that turns out best for you.

Mental Exercise For Bipolar Disorder

The brain is associated with all that we do and, similar to some other pieces of the body, it should be focused on as well.

Exercising the brain to further develop memory, concentration, or day-to-day usefulness is the first concern for some individuals, particularly as they progress in years. All things considered, individuals, everything being equal, can profit from integrating a couple of straightforward cerebrum practices into their day-to-day routines, which we'll investigate in more detail in this article.

Brain works out

Research has shown that there are numerous ways you can sharpen your smarts and assist your cerebrum with remaining sound, regardless of what age you are. Doing specific cerebrum activities to assist with supporting your memory, fixation, and focus can make day-to-day undertakings speedier and more straightforward to do, and keep your mind sharp as you progress in years.

We should make a more profound plunge into proof-based practices that offer the best brain-supporting advantages.

1. Play around with a jigsaw puzzle.
Whether you're assembling a 1,000-piece picture of the Eiffel Tower or joining 100 parts to make Mickey Mouse, dealing with a jigsaw puzzle is an incredible method for reinforcing your brain.
Research has shown that doing jigsaw puzzles selects numerous mental capacities and is a defensive variable for visuospatial mental maturation. At the end of the day, while assembling a jigsaw puzzle, you need to take a gander at various pieces and sort out where they fit inside the bigger picture. This can be an extraordinary method for testing and exercising your brain.

2. Take a shot at cards
When was the last time you played a round of cards? Specialists who led a focus in 2015 on intellectually animating exercises for grown-ups say a fast game can prompt more prominent cerebrum volume in a few districts of the mind. A similar report likewise found

that a round of cards could further develop memory and thinking abilities.

Have a go at learning one of these dependable games:
solitaire
span
Gin Rummy
Poker
hearts
insane eights

3. Build your vocabulary.
A rich vocabulary has an approach to making you sound brilliant. However, did you realize you can also transform a speedy jargon illustration into an invigorating cerebrum game?
Research shows that a lot more districts of the mind are engaged with jargon undertakings, especially in regions that are significant for visual and audible handling. To test this hypothesis, attempt this mental help action:
Keep a scratch pad with you when you read.
Record one new word, then look into the definition.
Attempt to utilize that word multiple times the following day.

4. Dance your heart out.
The Centers for Disease Prevention and Control note that learning new dance moves can expand your brain's handling velocity and memory. At the end of the day, get this party started on the dance floor and your brain will be much obliged.

Need to test it out? Check one of these dance exercises out:
Take a salsa, tap, hip-bounce, or contemporary dance class.
Attempt a Zumba or jazz practice class.
Watch an internet-based video with fun dance moves you've practically needed to learn.
Snatch an accomplice and learn a traditional dance.
Accumulate your companions and go line moving.

5. Utilize every one of your faculties
An examination report recommends that utilizing every one of your faculties might assist with reinforcing your cerebrum.
To give your faculties and your cerebrum an exercise, take a stab at doing exercises that at the same time connect every one of the five of your faculties. You could take a stab at baking a cluster of treats, visiting a rancher's market, or attempting another eatery while you center around smelling, contacting, tasting, seeing, and hearing all simultaneously.

6. Gain proficiency with another expertise
Mastering another expertise isn't just tomfoolery and fascinating, but it might likewise assist with reinforcing the associations in your brain.
Research likewise demonstrates the way that mastering another expertise can assist with further developing memory capability in more established grown-ups.
Is there something you've needed to figure out how to do practically forever? Maybe you might want to know how

to fix your vehicle, utilize a specific programming project, or ride a pony. You currently have another valid reason to discover that new expertise.

7. Show another expertise to another person.
One of the most mind-blowing ways of extending your mastery is to show your expertise to someone else.
After you gain proficiency with another expert, you want to rehearse it. Instructing it to another person expects you to make sense of the idea and right any slip-ups you make. For instance, figure out how to swing a golf club, then, at that point, show the moves toward a companion.

8. Pay attention to or play music.
Do you believe there should be a simple way to expand your innovative intellectual prowess? The response might lie in turning on some music.
As per a recent report, paying attention to cheerful tunes creates more imaginative arrangements compared with simply being peaceful. And that implies that turning up some great music can assist with helping your inventive reasoning and mental ability.
What's more, if you need to figure out how to play music, this present time is an extraordinary opportunity to begin because your mind is fit for mastering new abilities at any point in your life. That is the reason you're never too old to begin playing an instrument like the piano, guitar, or even drums.

9. Take another course.

Try not to become trapped in an endless cycle of your everyday errands. All things being equal, attempt better approaches to doing the same things.

Pick an alternate course to get to work every week or attempt an alternate method of transport, such as trekking or utilizing public transportation as opposed to driving. Your cerebrum can profit from this basic change, and you may be astounded by the fact that changing your thinking is so natural.

10. Think

Day-to-day contemplation can quiet your body, slow your breathing, and decrease pressure and nervousness.

Yet, did you have any idea that it might likewise help adjust your memory and increase your brain's capacity to process?

Track down a peaceful spot, shut your eyes and go through five minutes of contemplation every day.

11. Get familiar with another dialect

A survey has predominantly demonstrated the numerous mental advantages of having the option to communicate in more than one language.

As per various examinations, bilingualism can lead to better memory, improved visual-spatial abilities, and more elevated levels of inventiveness. Being familiar with more than one language may likewise assist you with exchanging all the more effectively between various assignments, and defer the beginning of age-related cognitive deterioration.

Fortunately, receiving the benefits of learning another language is rarely past the point of no return. As per scientists, you can help your memory and work on other mental capabilities by turning into an understudy of another dialect whenever you want in your life.

12. Take up Tai Chi.
It's a well-known fact that Tai Chi can help your well-being in numerous ways, including your psychological wellness. Additionally, it can likewise assist you with focusing when life appears to be out of equilibrium.
Taking up a normal act of Tai Chi can assist with diminishing pressure, improving sleep quality, and further developing memory. An examination found that drawn-out kendo training could prompt underlying changes in the cerebrum, bringing about an expansion in mind volume.
Fledglings truly do their best by taking a class to get familiar with the various developments. However, when you know the essentials, you can practice Tai Chi anywhere, whenever.

13. Focus on someone else.
The next time you connect with somebody, observe four things about them. Perhaps you notice the shade of their shirt or jeans. Is it safe to say that they are wearing glasses? Do they have a cap on, and providing that this is true, what sort of cap? What color is their hair?

When you settle on four things to recall, give them careful consideration and return to them later in the day. Record what you recall about those four subtleties.

Synopsis
Zeroing in on your mental well-being is quite possibly the most important thing you can manage to work on your fixation, concentration, memory, and mental spryness, regardless of what age you are.

By integrating cerebrum practices into your day-to-day existence, you'll get to challenge your brain, level up your mental abilities, and potentially gain some new useful knowledge and improve en route, as well.